CORNUCOPIA

CORNUCOPIA

✦

A JOURNEY THROUGH THE MOUNTAINS OF GOLD

A TRUE STORY BY LAUREL ANNE BRYAN

iUniverse, Inc.

New York Lincoln Shanghai

CORNUCOPIA
A JOURNEY THROUGH THE MOUNTAINS OF GOLD

iUniverse books may be ordered through booksellers or by contacting:

iUniverse
2021 Pine Lake Road, Suite 100
Lincoln, NE 68512
www.iuniverse.com
1-800-Authors (1-800-288-4677)

ISBN-13: 978-0-595-38480-8 (pbk)
ISBN-13: 978-0-595-82861-6 (ebk)
ISBN-10: 0-595-38480-3 (pbk)
ISBN-10: 0-595-82861-2 (ebk)

Printed in the United States of America

Dedicated to Spud…the hero in all my stories.

Contents

Acknowledgments

To Linda Thorpe: A heartfelt thank-you for your encouragement, support, and amazing grasp of the English language. Your faith in others is surpassed only by your gentle and graceful ways. I am eternally grateful.

To my dad, Jerry Bryan: Thank you for instilling in me the importance of family and preserving what we, as a people, cannot afford to lose. Thank you, also, for passing on your less than uncanny sense of direction. Had I not inherited your ability to get lost in my own backyard, I might have missed some of the most wonderful adventures of my life.

To my Mom, Lolah Yoshikawa: With every adventure came cuts, bruises, and broken bones. Thank you for patching up my wounds over the years. Your creativity with Vet Wrap puts even the most experienced medical professionals to shame.

To my grandma, Lillian Lowe: Thank you for whipping up one magical batch of green Jell-O.

Foreword

Gold was discovered in the small mining town of Cornucopia, Oregon, sometime around 1884. It is said its gold ore was so rich that nuggets would literally fall out of the rock, thus giving the town the name of Cornucopia: signifying wealth and plenty.

In the early 1900s, my grandparents, Emery Jennings Bryan and Alice Rose Aklin Bryan, purchased a small piece of ground in this once-bustling town. They built a cabin just off the banks of Pine Creek. Grandma planted two pine saplings: one on each side of the cabin's porch, which faced the creek.

Cornucopia is now a ghost town. My grandparents' cabin is long since gone. The only thing remaining of the original cabin is two towering pine trees standing guard over my family's heritage. I never knew my grandfather; he died when my own father was nine months old. My grandma often spoke of Grandpa and their life together so many years ago.

Even though I never saw the cabin or met the man, I have always felt a special bond with the land where they once stood. Pine Creek, Cornucopia, and the beautifully rugged Eagle Cap mountains hold a lifetime of memories for me.

I never panned for gold in its creeks or staked claim to its many mines, but wealth and plenty I certainly have derived from its bounty of heritage, adventure, and a magic which can not be bought with all the gold her mountains contain.

CORNUCOPIA: cor·nu·co·pi·a (kôr′nə-kō′pē-ə, -nyə-)
n.

1. Also called **horn of plenty**. Signifying wealth and plenty

2. *Greek Mythology.* The horn of the goat that suckled Zeus, which broke off and became filled with fruit. In folklore, it became full of whatever its owner desired.

3. An overflowing store; an abundance:

CORNUCOPIA

✦

A JOURNEY THROUGH THE MOUNTAINS OF GOLD

"Green Jell-O"

Wrapped in my grandma's worn terrycloth bathrobe, I sat at the kitchen table, mentally and physically exhausted, staring at a spoonful of green Jell-O. I don't think I have ever seen anything more insignificant, or more ridiculous, than those little, pie-shaped pieces of pineapple, suspended in a blob of florescent green gelatin. My grandpa use to say: "There's nothing like a spoon full of Jell-O to make you giggle when it wiggles." I think maybe he was right! This spoonful of Jell-O didn't have to wiggle; it didn't have to jiggle, or even move. What started out as a subtle grin soon developed into insuppressible giggles each time I glanced at the spoonful of green Jell-O staring up at me from my plate. It was only a matter of seconds before the giggles turned into insuppressible laughter. Tears streamed down my sunburned face as I tried to contain what was fast becoming an embarrassing case of hysterics. I couldn't tell if I was laughing or crying... probably both.

Five people sat around Grandma's kitchen table that afternoon: my mom; my grandma; my boyfriend, David; my son, Dillon; and me. Only David and Dillon could possibly understand what had come over me. Only the three of us knew what we had endured and how we came to be at my grandma's house in little Halfway, Oregon, the heart of Pine Valley.

PART I
The Journey

○ ○

One person's spoonful of green Jell-O may be another person's adventure of a lifetime.

—*L. A. B.*

It was Saturday morning, June 26, 2004, the second day of my vacation. I would have an entire week off from work. No phones, PDAs, pagers, or computers. No ringing, beeping, buzzing, or mysterious reboots for nine glorious days. Nine days to do anything I wanted, or nothing at all. My boyfriend, David, my son, Dillon, and I decided to pack into Pine Lakes. Dillon and I had packed into Pine Lakes the year before, but David had never been there. We decided to take a different route than before. We would start at Summit Point, make our way to Pine Lakes, and return by way of the steep, grueling trail that switched back and forth along Pine Creek, ending our trek at the Cornucopia Pack Station. We hoped the difference in elevation would make our ascent from Summit Point much less difficult than the switchbacks we conquered the year before. We later learned those switchbacks were appropriately dubbed the "Nip and Tuck." The hike would be longer, but the climb less severe. Pine Lakes—elevation: 7560 feet—can be found nestled deep within the Eagle Cap Wilderness, a stunning example of nature's most treasured creations.

We made arrangements with my father, Jerry Bryan, to move our truck from Summit Point to the pack station. I couldn't help thinking, "Man, I hope Dad doesn't forget to move the truck. It would certainly put a damper on the whole trip to walk all the way off the mountain, only to find we had no vehicle waiting for us on the other side." I could imagine Dad scratching his head and mumbling, "Oh, *that* pack station!"

We parked the truck at Summit Point and began strapping on packs full of carefully chosen gear. We had matches of all sorts and sizes: flimsy book matches, strike-anywhere matches, and those green waterproof matches that I swear must have to be wet before you can light them. You sure can't light them when they are dry. They remind me of childproof medicine bottles…the only people who can get them open *are* children. We packed various types of food, including packages of freeze-dried entrees, assorted flavors of instant oatmeal, a couple of military MREs (meals ready to eat), and a lifetime supply of instant potatoes ranging in flavors from butter and chives to herb and garlic.

Most importantly, I had my camera. For me this was the sole purpose of the entire trip. A $900 5 mega-pixel Olympus DC5050 with attachable lenses and filters ranging from polarized to UV. Oh, yeah! I placed the camera in a blue canvas fanny pack, bought specifically for the occasion, and strapped it securely around my waist. I could hardly wait to get started.

Even Spud, my 92-pound, white, German wirehaired pointer mix, seemed to anticipate my excitement. As I dropped the tailgate to the extended cab Dodge pickup, he easily jumped to the ground. The Rimadyl pills his vet prescribed seemed to be helping with the arthritis. I reached down to pet my big, beautiful, take-a-bullet-for-me dog. It is hard for me to admit that he is not a puppy anymore. Over the last few years, he has started showing his age. I think it is easier for me to accept my own ever-increasing age than it is to realize my loyal friend is ten, almost eleven years old…seventy in human years. He stood patiently while I strapped the extra-large dog pack to his back. Even with the Rimadyl pills contributing to his increased agility, I packed his load lighter. This year he would carry only his dog food and the first aid kit containing my expired bee-sting allergy kit. I wondered if an expired kit would do me any good if I actually got stung in the middle of the wilderness. I'd take it anyway. It was light enough. Besides, I think they put expiration dates on things just so you have to buy new ones.

With Spud properly packed, David, Dillon, and I flung our own packs across our backs. Were they this heavy last year? Surely not; but how could we pack any lighter? We would need every single item, including the little bottle of hair gel I had tucked away with my trial-sized shampoo and disposable razor.

So our ascent began on a crisp morning just after daybreak. It was a beautiful day: not too cold, but not too hot. A nice, cool breeze stayed with us most of the morning. "Man, these new packs sure are heavy. I don't think they fit us right. I wish we knew how they were supposed to fit. Are they supposed to ride low on your hips or high on your shoulders?" Dillon carried the pack I had used last year. It had ridden directly on top of my hips. By the time we had made it off the mountain, my hips were bruised and swollen. Not wanting a repeat of last year's discomfort, I purchased a new internal pack. This one sat higher on my shoulders—maybe too high, for it was hard to breathe.

We stopped beneath an old, gnarled ponderosa pine to take our first rest and check the elevation. My GPS read 6485 feet. We had come an entire one hundred yards. Already tired and breathing hard, I looked back toward Summit Point Lookout and was surprised to see a patch of snow, lying sheltered from the sun beneath a grove of pine trees. I didn't expect to see such a sight in late June. Good. The existence of snow meant an increase in water; and an increase in water meant the lakes would be filled to capacity. Last year's hike was in September, a few days before Labor Day. By then the hot sun had long since melted any remnants of snow, causing the lake to be half-empty…or half-full, depending on your outlook.

We took the time to nibble on a handful of tropical blend trail mix. It was here that we discovered Spud's fondness for honey-coated dehydrated oranges. Good, this would give me something in which to administer the Rimadyl he would take twice a day.

Now rested, we trudged on, following the trail along an old barbed-wire fence—the last remnant of anything resembling civilization. Another good mile and the trail crested a small hill overlooking a lush meadow. Smack-dab in the middle of the meadow lay a pond fed by an underground spring. Not until a year later would we learn the meadow's name: Little Eagle Meadows. Snow rimmed the west bank of the little pond. Bright sunlight reflecting from the waters' surface lay in complete contrast to the crisp, white snow that met the water's edge. I was overtaken by an urge to run barefoot through the snow. There were no thistles or stickers of any kind…nothing but lush, green grass, shallow water, and that rim of cold, white snow, hanging desperately to life before the oncoming summer robbed it of its form forever. Off went my shoes, and why not? There wasn't anyone to tell me it wasn't proper; and besides, I knew what my feet were about to undertake. It would do them some good to soak in the cold water. It says so right in my *Bradford Angier's Backcountry Basics*. Old Bradford himself said proper care of a person's feet is of utmost importance while hiking through the wilderness. The author goes on to say a good hiker, or poor lost soul, whichever the case may be, should stop and rest every twenty minutes, removing their shoes and soaking their feet in a cold stream whenever possible. I stripped my feet of shoes and socks and gingerly stepped into the ice-cold pond. Not even Spud was going to put his feet in that water! He watched me from shore with a look I can only describe as saying, "My human is an idiot."

David removed his pack and sat by the underground stream, playing with water skippers as Dillon took after the numerous frogs inhabiting the pond. Though my son made several attempts to bean one with his wrist rocket, he assures his toad-loving mom to this day that he missed every one. It is hard to believe he missed. I have seen the boy shoot a magpie in the head with a BB gun at thirty yards.

Once everyone was rested, we hoisted our packs up on our backs and took to the trail. After a few hundred yards, the trail began to wind its way up the first of many ridges. Good-bye, barbed wire. Good-bye, little pond. Good-bye, civilization. Our adventure had begun.

The trail wound us higher and higher up the ridge. When we reached the top, an hour from the little "frog pond," we were panting and out of breath. Each of us slung off our packs. David and Dillon reclined against a large boulder. Dillon pulled his hat down over his eyes. He reminded me of the cowboys in those old westerns. I didn't have a hat; I slathered on more SPF 50 sunscreen. I knew from experience how quickly the sun at high altitudes can redden even a person with my darker skin tone. I snapped a few pictures, looking back toward the direction we had come. You could barely make out the frog pond, with its little patch of white snow gleaming in the distance.

While the boys rested, Spud and I walked to the edge of the ridge to see if we could spot where the trail would pick up again. To say that "what lay ahead was something of a shock" would be an understatement. The ridge overlooked a huge bowl littered with pine trees and much more snow. So much snow, in fact, that it completely covered the trail. I walked back and forth along the ridge, trying to make out where the trail might be.

Soon David and Dillon joined me. David thought he saw part of the trail leading off the top side of the ridge, heading somewhat west. That didn't make sense to me, but I probably have the worse sense of direction known to man. Leaving his pack behind, David disappeared over the top edge of the ridge to look for the trail. Dillon and I waited seemingly forever on the rocks. We joked that David had been kidnapped by Bigfoot…never to be seen again. Dillon laughed, "It's more likely he wandered off after something with antlers and got himself lost." I could believe that theory since, next to new white socks and toilet paper, antlers are his favorite thing. But get lost? Not David. He was a walking compass. After we examined a few other ridiculous theories, David finally popped back over the ridge.

David discovered a trail heading west along the ridge. It appeared to wind around and head in the opposite direction of the lake. That might very well be. Many times last year, Dillon and I had checked the GPS to see where we were in relation to the lake. More than once the lake had actually been behind us as the trail wound its way around. At times the GPS had shown the lake at less than a quarter of a mile away as the crow flies, but still three or four miles away by trail. Oh, how sweet to be a crow at a time like this. My GPS! I forgot I had it! I still had Pine Lakes marked from last year's hike. I took the GPS out of my pack and started walking back and forth across the ridge. For some stupid reason, you have to be walking at least 1.2 miles an hour before the GPS can get an accurate reading. Who comes up with this stuff? Watching the little arrow, I wandered around in a tight circle, trying to maintain the proper speed while finding our bearing. There. The needle pointed to the northeast, the opposite direction of the trail David had seen. We assumed there must be two trails and agreed to head on into the snow-covered bowl.

Without an actual trail to follow, we took a more direct route down into the bowl, side-hilling ridges of snow as we went. At times the snow made it difficult. If you lost your footing, you would slide toward the bottom of the bowl and have to start back up, sometimes waist deep in snow. It was a pain, but not impossible nor dangerous. Now and then the trail would emerge from a bare spot where the snow had melted, giving us a glimpse of hope that, indeed, we were going in the right direction. Again, I was surprised at the sight of so much snow. I assumed it would have long since melted. I couldn't have been more wrong.

We continued along the edge of the bowl, fighting patches of snow as we went. Several hours later we had made our way across the bowl to the opposite ridge. I glanced at Dillon's face as he looked back over our trail. He hated the whole thing. I could tell. You didn't have to be a mind reader to know he was thinking he would rather be doing just about anything other than trudging up a mountain with 50 pounds strapped to his back. David didn't look much better. He is a little harder to read; but the quiet, almost restrained look in his eye told me he hated it, too. I didn't like feeling responsible for their discomfort. What did they expect? Dillon had hiked with me before. Other than the addition of some unexpected snow, this particular route was actually less severe than the route we took last year. Still, I did feel responsible for their misery, and I hated it. I didn't mind the hike, the steep hills, and waist-deep snowdrifts. I didn't mind the hot sun beating down on the top of my dark hair. I didn't even mind the ill-fitting pack that dug into my shoulders and bruised my hips. What I hated was worrying about everyone else's discomfort and feeling responsible for it. There wasn't anything I could do about it now; besides, I didn't force either one of them to come. I could have easily gone by myself...and would have.

Each of us stood atop the ridge and looked down into yet another bowl, scattered with even larger areas of snow. The horizon was notched with two saddles sitting opposite each other on the rim across from us. We could barely make out the trail as it zigzagged its way up the hill from one saddle to the next, and back again. There was no way of knowing through which saddle the trail would lead. David checked his watch: 8:30 PM. It would be dark in less than an hour. I wanted to kick myself for choosing this route. I had no idea how far we were from the lake, or even if we had taken the right trail. I turned my face upward. The bleak, cloud-covered sky mirrored my darkening mood. We needed to find a place to camp for the night, and fast. If the sky was any indication, it was likely to rain. Great, just what we needed. There was no way I was going to pitch a tent on the top of the ridge. By the looks of the clouds, I feared they contained much more than rain or even snow. I had no intention of being the tallest thing on the mountain.

We walked down into the bowl, looking for a good spot to set up camp for the night. Near the bottom of the bowl, the trail came to a fork. Placed at the fork was an old sign in the shape of a cross. Barely legible were the words: Crater Lake, 8 miles; Pine Lakes, 5 miles. It might as well have read: Here lie three really stupid people and a big dog. We could only assume that we were closer to Pine Lakes than we were to Crater Lake. An even bigger assumption was which fork went to which lake. Again I glanced up at the darkening sky. More rain clouds joined the others. We needed to set up camp soon, or we would be setting up in the rain.

We walked another quarter of a mile before it became apparent there would be no ideal spot to set up camp. We were no longer in the bottom of the bowl, but had started ascending the other side. This meant finding a flat spot was all but impossible. The only semi-flat spot clear of snow was right smack in the middle of the trail. The ground was soaked from melting snow that trickled down the side of the mountain, searching for the lowest ground in which to form puddles.

Dillon and I pulled out the little two-man bivy tent and proceeded to assemble our shelter for the night. David had brought only a piece of plastic to use as his tent. The plastic wasn't even the good kind. This plastic was that flimsy, light stuff a person might use to cover a casserole! David had brought Saran wrap instead of a tent. To this day I have no idea what he was thinking. Why he didn't bring a real tent is beyond me. One thing I do know…he will never make that mistake again.

There wasn't a minute to spare between the time our shelters went up and darkness consumed the night sky. Spud lay just outside the head of our tent. Dillon and I were crammed into the bivy tent like sardines. "Two-man" was a stretch of the imagination. You might get two people in one coffin, but who would want to! This tent reminded me of a nylon coffin: barely six feet long, bigger at the head and tapering off toward your feet.

I don't remember the ground ever being this hard. I could feel every little rock and twig beneath my sleeping bag. Dillon, on the other hand, seemed to be snug as a bug in a rug. Soon all I could hear was his heavy breathing and a low, distant rumble, rolling slowly across the night sky. I adjusted my pistol, flashlight, and knife within reach. The pistol was for protection against ax murderers and cougars that might be roaming the wilderness, prowling for their next victim. The flashlight was needed in case I had to find the tent's zipper in the middle of the night. The knife was insurance, just in case I couldn't find the flashlight. I have a little problem with claustrophobia and confined spaces…such as tents. If I couldn't find the zipper, I'd cut my way out. With my gear laid out and the location of the zipper burned into my brain, I closed my eyes and prayed for sleep.

Moments later it began. With a splat…splat…plop, heavy drops of rain pelted the top of the tent. The third drop brought Spud diving for the small opening I had left in the tent door. He smelled like a dog and shed profusely, but I didn't argue. It was comforting to have my big guardian close by. Seconds later more rain fell, accompanied by even louder rumbling. Soon the distant rumble turned into deafening explosions of thunder, as if shot from the barrel of cannon, directly over our heads. The rain, no longer distinguishable as drops, came in buckets, as if poured from the night sky.

It could have been three minutes or three hours before it dawned on me: David was out *in the storm,* wrapped in his little piece of Saran wrap. What kind of girlfriend thought of her dog's well-being before that of her man? I think I hesitated for a few more seconds. How would he fit? I wasn't about to send my dog back out in that storm just because the guy wasn't prepared. Besides, it was his own fault; he had chosen to bring a roll of Saran wrap instead of paying thirty bucks for a real tent. I called out his name. "David?" He didn't hear me at first over the booming thunder. "David, how are you doing out there?" *What kind of a question is that? What did I expect him to say?* "Are you getting wet?" Another profound inquiry on my part. I sincerely hoped that, by some miraculous feat, he was tucked up under a tree, dry as a bone, and I wouldn't have to kick my dog out to make room for him. After all, why should poor planning on his part constitute an emergency at the expense of my puppy! I didn't have to ask again. Of course, he was not OK. David crawled into the tent, dragging his rain-soaked sleeping bag behind him. He was a mess. Shivering from the cold, David curled up into a ball at the head of the tent. The dome-shaped pop-out was barely big enough for the six feet two, 240-pound drowned rat. Spud, who appeared to be making himself as small and inconspicuous as possible, seemed to vanish farther back into the cramped little tent. He must have thought if nobody noticed him, he wouldn't be tossed out into the storm. Later we would be glad to have him in the tent with us. A big, smelly dog was a warm dog, nonetheless.

More than once during the night, lightning seemed to strike within inches of our tent. I counted the amount of time that lapsed between the deafening cracks of thunder and the flashes of lightning that followed. "One, one thousand…two, one thousand…" *Crrrrack!* Thunder echoed through the canyon like a high-powered rifle. You could no longer distinguish the time between the sound of thunder and flashes of lightning. Each flash lit the inside of our tent with an explosion of light that left us temporarily blinded. The wind howled and whipped at the walls of our little tent. I feared the tent would be ripped apart at any moment. Without our combined body weight to hold it down, I am sure our tent would have ended up somewhere over the rainbow, with a dead witch under it. "Spud, I don't think we're in Kansas anymore."

Neither David nor I slept a wink. I prayed we wouldn't be struck by lightning, crushed to death by a falling tree, or swept away by a flash flood. I used to like thunderstorms, or so I thought. That is easy to say from the comfort of your own home. It is like listening to music on the radio, where you control the volume to your liking, versus being smack-dab in the middle of a live rock concert with your head inches from massive speakers. We were part of a heavy metal concert, with no way of seeking shelter from its violent symphony.

3:30 AM brought with it relief from the night's vicious tantrum. Exhausted and sore, we crawled out of the tiny tent. We stood in a tight circle, reading each other's expressions. It was still dark, but there was no doubt what each of us was thinking. We all just wanted to go home. We built a small fire to cook our breakfast and dry out some of the gear. Not wanting to stay in this spot a moment longer, we opted to pack our gear wet and get to the lake. Once there we could spread everything out and let it dry properly. Dillon stomped-out the remaining campfire while ceremoniously christening the spot: Satan's Camp from Hell. Without a second look back, the four of us slowly made our way as far from Satan's Camp as we could.

The crisp air of daybreak led us into more and more snow with every step we took. The trail was obliterated. According to my GPS, the lake was just over the saddle to the east. Going by way of the trail would not be possible. It would mean miles of trudging through deep snow as the trail zigzagged its way across the mountain between saddles. We decided to take a shortcut and climb straight up into the nearest saddle. If we were reading the GPS correctly, the saddle should lie just above the lakes.

Climbing straight up with the added hindrance of deep snow would have been difficult enough; but lying awake on a hard, cold, unforgiving ground the night before made it damn near unbearable. You had to pull yourself up, one step at a time, never knowing when you might break through the snow. Less then a quarter of the way up the mountain, my legs turned to noodles, and my right knee gave out. The climb proved equally as difficult for Spud. The weight of his pack pulled him over backward. He whimpered from the pain in his hips. I wanted so badly to pick him up and carry him. I could no more carry the 92-pound dog than fly. I reached down and released the buckles to his pack. I could at least carry that. Free from his pack, Spud could have easily gone on ahead. Instead, he stayed with me every step of the way, allowing me to use him as support when I lost my footing. More than once he got just above me, dug his feet into the snow, and allowed me to grab onto his collar to help pull myself up another step. If anyone could have witnessed the concern and unadulterated compassion the dog showed for his human, they would never question why he is allowed to sleep inside the tent on a stormy night.

David and Dillon had almost reached the top. Just above them, standing atop the ridge like a sentry, was a lone pine tree full of grouse! We were going to have grouse for dinner! The thought of roasted bird, seasoned with lemon pepper, renewed my climb. On all fours, I scurried up the hill to catch up with the boys. I held Spud back to prevent him from flushing the birds. Dillon grabbed for his wrist rocket and fumbled for the shot he carried in his pocket. By the time he took aim, the grouse were gone. It would be MREs and instant potatoes for dinner again. Note to self: next trip, bring the .410.

David and Dillon reached the saddle. I watched them both as they stood atop the ridge, looking out across another snow-covered bowl. I recognized the look of awe on their faces as they took in the spectacular view before them. The pristine, blue waters of Pine Lakes, the most beautiful place on God's green earth, lay nestled at the bottom of the snow covered bowl. Patches of broken ice floated calmly in vivid blue water as brilliant white snow framed a lake mirroring the fluffy, white clouds and blue sky above. Pine Lakes is actually two lakes, with the larger pouring into the smaller. The two lakes then form the beginning of Pine Creek, which flows down the Eagle Caps, through the old Cornucopia ghost town, and on toward the little town of Halfway, Oregon. The creek winds for miles, passing my grandpa Emmett's old house in Oxbow, where it eventually pours into the Snake River. I could have died right there on the spot, and died the happiest person in the world. We had made it. We had almost made it.

After taking in the view and contemplating the meaning of life, we soon realized our journey was not over. We were still quite a distance from the lake. This last bowl would prove to be more treacherous than those previous. This time, instead of climbing up, we would have to go down. The outer walls of the bowl were practically vertical. There was no sign of the trail; it had long been buried under who knows how much snow. The only indication of its depth was the realization that the little tree Spud had just peed on was not a little tree, but the top of a really big tree. I walked back and forth along the top of the ridge, searching for a place to descend. I thought to myself, "Nobody is going to believe this. I had better snap some pictures." I shot a few pictures of the lakes below. I turned back and took pictures of Dillon, standing atop a large cornice. The cap of snow curled around like a giant Hershey's Kiss. It reminded me of the mountain where the Grinch lived in Dr. Seuss's book, *The Grinch Who Stole Christmas*. Dillon did not know he was actually standing on a huge overhang of snow. A few more feet, and he could slide off and not stop until he ended up in the lake. Now I understood which side of the mountain was the lee side and why you should never set camp under it.

Rested up and pictures taken, it was time to figure out how to get down to the lake. From our vantage point, we marked out a route that would take us in the right direction while avoiding a pool of frozen slush that lay in a little meadow just above the lake. The spring runoff had pooled there, creating a giant, half-frozen slushy. If we fell in the slushy, I doubted we would be found until the first thaw.

Going down the mountain was harder for me than going up! My knee would no longer support me. The heavy pack pulled me over backward as Dillon and I tried to scale our way around a vertical bluff jutting out from under the snow. It soon became clear there was no way I was getting across with my pack on. Dillon graciously took my pack, along with his own, and headed toward David, who was already halfway down the slope. How did David get down so fast? I clung to whatever I could to avoid skating down the mountain out of control. More than once my dog and I both lost our grip and found ourselves skidding down through the snow. Spud and I took turns preventing the other from becoming a live toboggan. When we met up with Dillon, I took my pack from him, but didn't put it on. Why fight it? I was already soaked, and I didn't feel like walking another step. I decided to slide the rest of the way down the mountain on my butt. Just at the top of the slush pond, there was a small ridge of rocks. I hoped that if I went out of control in their direction, these rocks would stop me from sliding into the slushy water. In my opinion taking a chance on broken bones was better then drowning. Anything was better then drowning. Tying the pack to my belt, I sat down on my butt, kicked up my feet, and was off down the mountain like a human bobsled. It wasn't nearly as graceful as I imagined. Spud could easily have trotted down the mountain. Instead, my goofy dog chose to run alongside me, occasionally grabbing at a pant leg or part of my pack. We were a spinning mass of flailing arms, legs, pack, and dog, snowballing down the mountain. We managed to reach the bottom, avoiding both the pond of slush and the rocks. Breathless, we floundered at the bottom of the slope, looking like a couple of disheveled snow angels. Spud stood up and shook the snow from his coat. I sat up and looked back at the path we had made in the snow, "That was invigorating, but let's *not* do it again, OK, dog?" The slide down the mountain had sealed our fate. There was no going back. No one, not even a dog, would be able to walk back out the way we came.

Now at the bottom of the snow-covered slope, we still had some distance to cover before reaching the lake. A smaller bowl sat nestled inside the one we just bobsledded down. This smaller bowl cupped the lake. Spring runoff trickled down the sides of the bowl to form the lakes below. By the looks of it, Pine Valley was going to have plenty of water this year! David and Dillon were nowhere in sight. Apparently they had found the trail that would take them around to the front side of the lake. Being this close to the lake meant denser forest. I could not see the lake from here. I knew we were on the backside and just above it. I also knew how steep it was from the ridge to the lake. In previous years I had camped at the base of the vertical wall, which plunged a good four hundred feet to the water. Spud and I would have to walk completely around the lake and come at it from the other direction. The snow was able to support my weight. Both Spud and I could walk on top without falling through. From the looks of David and Dillon's tracks, they weren't as lucky. The size of the holes they left in the snow indicated they must have broken through up to their waist at times. What a bummer that must have been! I couldn't help but grin. It served them right for taking off without me. Spud and I continued following their tracks around the lake, sometimes walking, sometimes sledding down the many snow-covered bluffs.

An hour later we arrived together at the lake. We were no longer amazed at how much of the area was covered in snow. Right next to the water, we found a small bare patch to make camp. There was not a dry spot to be found. This was as good as it was going to get. We unpacked our gear and spread everything out for the sun to dry. For as much snow as there was, it really was not that cold. The sky was clear, and the sun felt hot on our heads. There was plenty of time to dry our things and set up camp for the night. Not wanting a repeat of the night before, David took extra care to build a shelter. Much to the dismay of the environmentally conscious, we defaced a few saplings and managed to create a fairly sound shelter to protect him from the elements. David spent the rest of the day fishing. Dillon stayed in camp and rummaged through his supplies. This was Dillon's heaven. As a little boy, he had often admired the transient "bag man." Having the ability to carry everything Dillon needed on his back, with various gadgets and tools at his disposal, was indeed his idea of heaven. I always thought my oldest boy would make a great turtle.

Spud and I took off exploring and shooting pictures of the area. I managed to get the ultimate picture of Spud overlooking the lake. I had always wanted a decent picture of my dog, and this was perfect. I snapped several shots as he stood in profile, gazing out over the water in seemingly deep doggy thoughts. This was most certainly a Kodak moment if ever there was one. We wandered toward the head of the lake, to the trail that would eventually lead us home. I wanted to get a perspective of what lay ahead. A sweeping view of the mountains toward home could be seen while standing on the tallest mass of rock. From what I could see, there was very little snow. Our trip home should prove uneventful. I snapped a few more pictures, and headed back to camp.

Later that afternoon I decided to take a bath. Yes, it would be cold; but after spending the night in a tent with a wet dog, it would be worth it. I shed my trail clothes and stepped gingerly into the icy water that separated the two lakes. After my feet went numb, the rest wasn't so bad…really. Spud sat on shore, head cocked and ears perked slightly up. There was that look again: "My human is an idiot." When I was just getting comfortable with the idea of not being seen, a low-flying Cessna circled overhead. The pilot must have thought he had stumbled on a family of Bigfoot. No humans in their right minds would be up here this time of the year.

It rained again that night, but nothing like the downpour from the storm that assaulted us the night before. The light, steady rain drumming the top of our tent soothed me to sleep almost immediately. I do not think the two Tylenol PM I took just before bed hurt either. David managed to stay dry under his make-shift shelter, and everyone slept the entire night.

We decided not to stay another day. We weren't prepared for the conditions we encountered, and were pretty much done with the whole thing. We took the time to dry and neatly pack our belongings. By 10:00 AM we were heading back toward civilization. We had somewhat of a difficult time getting across the creek that poured directly out of the lake. You either had to cross a narrow concrete dam about eight inches wide, or wade across the waist-deep water. Since having knee surgery, my balance is no longer what it used to be. So I handed my pack to Dillon, dismissed the concrete wall, and waded across. Spud tried to follow by way of the narrow concrete wall and lost his footing. Dillon grabbed him around the torso just as he started over the edge. He tossed the big dog like a sack of potatoes to safety on the other side. David went next, taking great pains to keep his feet dry. I had to smile at his futile attempts. We stood on the opposite side and waited for Dillon to change his wet socks. Somehow my camera slipped off my arm and started rolling down the bank. It would have ended up in the creek had David not speared it with his walking stick. Thank goodness for the man's catlike reflexes. The thought of losing my camera and the pictures it contained was enough to give me chills. Not wanting to take a chance on dropping my camera again, I hung it around my neck, where it would stay for the remainder of the hike.

Compared to the hike in, the absence of snow made the descent toward home seem like a walk in the park. The heavy packs pulled at our shoulders, our feet ached, and we were exhausted. But we were heading home. I snapped more pictures as we meandered our way down the trail, zigzagging from one cutback to another. Water from the melting snow had turned the trail into a miniature riverbed. A good two inches of water ran steadily down the entire trail. So much for David's dry feet!

There were fewer patches of snow, and only one presented any kind of a real challenge. The snow formed a huge tunnel over a natural spring fingering its way from the top of the mountain all the way to Pine Creek below. In certain spots you could see the water flowing twelve to fifteen feet beneath the tunnel. There was no way around; we would have to go over it. It was creepy thinking you might break through and end up trapped under the tunnel of snow, or lose your footing and end up sliding all the way to the bottom. We each side-hilled our way across this last obstacle of snow. Spud slowed his natural pace and walked with me, step for step, helping me keep my balance. I reached down and patted his furry, white head, "Lassie's got nothing on you, pooch."

This side of the mountain was familiar to Dillon and me. We recognized trees, bushes, and favorite little resting areas where we stopped the year before. We came up on a spring, barely recognizable as the same little spring where we had filled our water bottles the year before. With the abundance of melting snow, the spring was now filled to capacity. We passed the dead snag, which served as a marker for the wilderness boundary. The path led us through another wooded area. It reminded me of a hobbit's trail, lined in huckleberry bushes. Toward the bottom of the canyon, the trail weaved through a small, dense forest of pine trees. Once again, snow clung to life in this shaded area and covered the trail. It took some time to gather our bearings before we picked up the trail leading out of the dense maze.

Soon we reached the red footbridge, crossing Pine Creek once more. There was the old piece of rusted mining equipment that caused me to reflect on the days when this entire mountain was alive with prospectors in search of gold. What a life they must have lived! We, with our fancy, ergonomically designed packs and walking sticks, trekking through the woods for fun, were no comparison to the hardy men and women who lived and survived out here as a way of life. I both admired and envied them.

The trail leveled as it ran along Pine Creek toward the bottom of the canyon. Another two miles should find us at the truck I hoped was waiting to take us home. I could not help but notice how full the creek was compared to last year. With all the melting snow and rain, I guess that would be expected. I tried to encourage David and Dillon by telling them how close we were to the truck. We only had to follow the creek a little longer before crossing one last time, where the old bridge was removed.

Everyone was beat, but we trudged on toward the end of our adventure. Images of Washington's troops at Valley Forge flashed through my mind. OK, so maybe I have a bit of an overactive imagination. Still, we really were a vision of despair.

Dillon had gone ahead. Thinking it might lighten the mood, I joked to David, "Wouldn't it be a bummer if we got all the way to the end, and couldn't cross the creek?" I should learn to keep my mouth shut.

Less than a quarter of a mile brought us to the torn-out bridge. Dillon's back was to us as he sat on his haunches, head in his hands, staring into the water. My heart sank when I realized the source of his dismay. Little Pine Creek had transformed into a raging river. The water gushed downstream in a deafening roar. Things didn't look so good from this point, but there was still hope. You were not supposed to cross at this spot, anyway. About one hundred yards upstream from the bridge, the trail veered off to a shallow area where people and horses normally crossed. We headed back up the trail, to the actual crossing. It was not as deep here, but appeared to be as swift. We walked up and down the creek for what seemed like hours, trying to find an easy place to cross. I hoped for a spot narrow enough to jump, or for a fallen tree on which to cross. There was nothing. Not one of us could swim, and all were equally terrified of the water. It seemed hopeless. We couldn't go on, and we couldn't go back. I wondered how long it would be before somebody used this trail and found us perched on the bank, staring longingly at the opposite shore.

After several failed attempts, David finally crossed by tying off a rope to a pine tree upstream. With a walking stick in one hand, and a death grip on the rope, David inched his way across the creek, landing safely on the opposite bank. Dillon and I looked at each other with dread. Oh, God…it was our turn.

We thought it might be easier to cross if we did not have the packs. I removed my pistol and GPS from my pack. I then removed my digital camera from where it hung around my neck. I did not want to chance dumping them in the creek. Using the rope like a trolley cable, we slid the packs across one at a time. Dillon tossed my gun and GPS over to David with ease. He offered to toss my camera, but I did not want to risk it. I would throw it across in the hope that David would catch it before it hit the ground. The thought crossed my mind that I should take the memory card out and carry it in my teeth. I knew I had some nice pictures and did not want to lose them even if the camera broke. I shrugged off the idea and steadied myself to toss the camera. With the camera zipped snuggly in a fanny pack, I held the pack by the strap. I looked over at David on the other side, "OK…on the count of three…One…" Again the thought crossed my mind to remove the film. "Two…" Should I be tossing this across underhand by the strap? "Three!" From the moment the camera left my hand, it felt wrong. Tossing the bag underhand sent it soaring straight up in the air, directly between David and me. It was like watching a train wreck in slow motion. I watched my camera soar high into the air, spin around a few times, and drop from the sky, right into the raging creek. It hit the water at the same time my heart stopped. I watched the blue fanny pack drift back and forth, from one side of the creek to the other, just beyond the reach of any would-be rescuer. Dillon almost had it once. The camera floated teasingly close to where he lay, outstretched on his belly. It passed just inches from his fingertips. I raced down the edge of the creek, hoping the strap would snag on the bank. I could not run far. High water obliterated the bank, leaving nothing but a mass of impenetrable bushes and vegetation. In what seemed like an eternity, but was more likely a matter of seconds, the current carried my camera and our entire adventure downstream. I could not even cry; I wanted to, but I could not. I was numb. It was gone. All of it was gone. The pictures of the beautiful lake, those of Dillon standing on the edge of the cornice, and of Spud overlooking the lake…gone. Nobody was going to believe our tales of adventure. The proof was hurling down the creek, headed for the Snake River. I would have to kick myself later; Dillon and I were still on the wrong side of the creek. And it was getting dark.

I headed back to where Dillon and David waited, each afraid to say anything to me. I suppose they thought I would snap. I did not. It was my own fault: I should have let Dillon toss the camera across; I should have thrown it overhand; I should have taken the memory card out and carried it in my teeth. I should have, but I did not. I would worry about all that tomorrow. Right now I needed to figure out how to get Dillon and myself across that creek.

Dillon decided to go next. He crossed in the same spot as David had. I watched from shore in complete and utter terror. As he inched his way closer and closer to the middle of the raging creek, my mind raced with images of him falling and being swept downstream, just beyond my reach. I would be just as helpless to save him as I was the camera. The images made me sick to my stomach. I do not think it mattered whether we could swim or not. The water was moving so fast. I doubt Mark Spitz could have gotten out if the current took hold. Every inch took Dillon farther into the creek…farther from my ability to reach out and save him. Inch by inch, he pulled himself closer to the opposite side of the creek and, finally, to safety.

The next challenge would be getting Spud across. He would try to go with me, and in his loyalty, he would more likely become a hindrance. Even if he tried to cross on his own, the current was too strong. I cinched his collar tight around his neck. I tied the orange nylon rope

David and Dillon had used to his collar, and tossed the slack to David. Dillon and David began urging Spud across the creek. Spud looked back at me with sad, brown eyes that broke my heart. I looked over at David and Dillon, "Don't you dare let go of him...not for anything." I could bear losing my camera; I might even get over losing my boyfriend. But not my dog. I said a quick prayer, "Dear God...not my dog...take the camera...take anything...but don't take my dog." David and Dillon quickly pulled Spud across the creek and removed the rope.

I breathed a sigh of relief, however fleeting, since I would be next. I grabbed hold of the rope and tried to cross in the same spot. I just couldn't do it. Each step brought the raging water higher and higher up my legs. I was not tall enough for the water to flow between my legs, like David and Dillon. Once it reached my torso, the force of the current was too strong; I could not keep my feet on the bottom. I had to turn back. I sat on the creek bank, pitifully alone and feeling quite sorry for myself. "I guess you will have to come back for me in late spring, after the water subsides. Don't worry, I'll still be here. Just toss me a little trail mix and a flashlight." It was hopeless. How was I ever going to get across that creek? I thought about taking a big run at it and jumping across. I would get wet, but if I landed just the other side of the middle, Dillon and David might be able to catch me before I drowned. I even tried to talk them into going on without me, and bringing a horse back to ride across, or sending a helicopter back for me. A helicopter would be cool. It was getting darker by the minute, and the ideas, more ridiculous by the second.

Enough was enough. I untied the rope from where David and Dillon had used it, and tied it to a tree farther upstream. It was wider here but did not look as deep. I could tell David thought I was crazy for crossing here. To his credit he did not say a word. I suppose he thought that if I considered it a better spot, I would muster enough courage to cross. While Dillon held Spud, I stepped into the creek. I found if I did not lift my feet off the bottom, the current did not jerk my legs out from under me. I slowly shuffled farther out into the creek. The death grip on the rope burned my hands. Water inched its way farther and farther up my legs, not quite reaching my torso. One hundred years later, I reached the other side. Exhaling the breath I had been holding, I dropped to my knees and was immersed in dog kisses, from one side of my face to the other.

The four of us stood on the same side of the creek at last, tired and wet from the waist down, but relieved to be standing on solid ground. Our feelings of elation over having avoided the wrath of Mother Nature were short-lived. For at that very moment, the sky opened and began pouring sheets of rain from its angry bowels. Drenched from the downpour, we scurried to gather our packs, and made a dash to the truck we hoped was parked a mile from where we stood. Even as tired and miserable as we were, our spirits seemed to lift. Maybe it was because we knew our ordeal was at an end. We had made it, no matter what Mother Nature had thrown at us. Through intense thunderstorms, massive snowdrifts, and the relentless, pouring rain, we had made it. There was still the possibility Dad might have forgotten to move our truck from Summit Point to the pack station. Not wanting to jinx us again, I kept the thought to myself. Fortunately, Dad did not forget, and we found the Dodge waiting for us, reminiscent of a noble white steed on wheels. We tossed our junk (no longer referred to as gear) into the truck bed and dropped the tailgate for Spud, who dove for the shelter of his travel carrier. With the Eagle Caps in the rearview mirror, our wet faces pointing toward home, and no mention of a lost camera, we soon found ourselves on Granny's doorstep.

Granny opened the door to find three drowned rats and a wet dog. She escorted us inside and began preparations to dry us out. Dillon and David managed to find clean, dry clothes in their packs. I jumped in the shower while Grandma washed and dried the clothes I had been wearing. Wrapped in Grandma's soft terrycloth bathrobe, I sat down at the kitchen table with my mom. While Grandma whipped up a generous batch of homemade spaghetti to feed the starving troops, David,

Dillon, and I tried, in vain, to recount the trials of our three-day adventure. Our recollection of the events felt insignificant compared to the actual experience. I had the feeling Mom and Grandma just didn't get it. Without experiencing it first hand, maybe they never would. I'm sure to those listening; our adventure seemed as distant and far away as the lake itself…as unassuming as that jiggling spoonful of florescent green Jell-O seemed to me.

PART II
Search for the Camera

o o o o o o o o o o o o o o o o o o o o o o o o o o o o o o o o o

Sometimes the end of the trail is only the beginning of the journey.

—L. A. B.

July 10, 2004: The old Dodge jerked us side-to-side as it bounced over large rocks and potholes. Rough, dusty, and full of large ruts, the narrow mountain road leading to the Pine Lakes trailhead was barely wide enough for the half-ton truck. I pulled to the side and parked under the same pine tree where the truck had waited for us three weeks earlier. David and I decided to start our search at the exact spot where I had thrown my camera in the creek. I had spent three weeks kicking myself everyday, wondering how I could have done something so stupid. I might as well have walked up to the creek, taken the camera from around my neck, and gently tossed it into the water, calling it an offering to the gods of stupidity. Every day, thoughts of how I should have done it differently tormented me. I should have thrown it overhand. I should have let Dillon throw it across. I should have done many things…but I didn't. Instead, I sent a $900 camera soaring straight up into the air, and watched helplessly as it landed in the midst of whitewater rapids…our entire adventure, carried away by the raging current.

Pine Creek looked nothing like it did that fateful day three short weeks ago. Where once the water engulfed the banks in a roaring torrent, it now rolled gently over rocks and under fallen trees. Water barely reached halfway up the creek's bank. We could easily cross almost anywhere we wanted.

We reached the end of the trail, where it crossed the creek, and started our search for the lost camera. David went down one side of the creek; Spud and I, the other. Each of us zigzagged, back and forth, meeting in the middle before returning to our own side. Even though the water level was now half of what it had been, there were still holes over my head. It seemed hopeless. If the camera had not made it clear to the Snake River by now, it could be anywhere. It could be in any number of holes too deep to see the bottom. It could be under a washed-out area of the bank, or under a fallen tree. We tried to cover every inch, but there were too many variables. If you missed a square inch, you might as well have missed the entire creek. I had hoped that the camera bag snagged itself on a limb, and would be sitting there waiting for me. I even thought that maybe somebody might find it. Maybe they would find my name on the fishing license tucked away in one of the compartments, and would return it. I did not expect the camera to be any good; but in the back of my mind, I hoped the pictures would be salvageable. I had spent hours on the Internet, searching for information on picture cards. I looked in forums to see if anybody else had experienced something similar and what the outcome had been. Several newsgroups told of stories where a person had dropped their camera in the water, and the pictures were still good. Although the stories gave me hope, I knew being underwater for a few seconds and being under for three weeks were two entirely different things. Still, we searched for the camera until we could no longer stand the cold water. Just before dark, we called it quits and headed home. Cold and disappointed, I would find no comfort in the less than encouraging words of others: "You're not going to find the camera…it's either busted into a million pieces, or all the way to the Pacific Ocean by now."

PART III
The Search Continues

o o o o o o o o o o o o o o o o o o o o o o o o o o o o o o o o o o

Persistence can often lead to obsession if not mixed with a healthy dose of determination and a little luck.

—L. A. B.

September 10, 2004: I pulled the little camp trailer down a bumpy, dusty dirt road that wound through Cornucopia Township. Carefully I turned down the steep, boulder-lined road that led into my family's old homestead along Pine Creek. My twelve-year-old son, Blake, and his cousin, Garet, sat next to each other in the back seat of the truck. Blake and Garet wanted to camp and fish for the weekend. I went along as chauffeur and cook. The boys explored the creek and fished while I set up camp. I found myself staring longingly in the direction of Pine Lakes trailhead. Another whole month had passed, and still I could not get that camera out of my mind. Even if I wanted to, friends and co-workers would not allow it. "Hey, Laurie, throw any $900 digital cameras in the creek lately?" Everybody is a comedian.

Spud sat beside me on a big boulder protruding from the waters edge. The top of the rock formed a perfect spot to sit. From the time I was little, I remember sitting on the same big rock, fishing, soaking my bare feet, or sitting in silence, listening to soothing sounds of the creek. This was, and will always be, one of my favorite spots on earth. Knees tucked up under my chin, I stared into the water. Perhaps I hoped that if I stared long and hard enough, my lost camera would come floating by on a magic carpet of gently moving current. Spud's cold, wet nose against my cheek brought me abruptly back to reality. I couldn't stand it! I had to search for the camera again. I was this close. What would it hurt?

Shortly after breakfast the next morning, the boys and I, along with Spud, drove to the pack station. We would start near the same place David and I had given up our search. We carefully made our way, through thick brush and vegetation, to the banks of Pine Creek. The creek had less water in it than it did a month earlier. Even the deepest holes were shallow enough to see the bottom. More of the bank was exposed. Nevertheless, searching was harder without another person. The boys were not at all interested in searching for a stupid camera that was probably ruined anyway.

I let the boys fish. Back into the water I went, crossing from one side of the creek to the other. Spud looked confused, as if he found it perplexing why a person would walk back and forth across slippery rocks when you could easily walk the bank. Still, he followed my every step. I reached into every dark and murky hole the forces of erosion had cut into the bank. I was wet up to my neck. There were so many places where a camera could get entangled. I explored every one I could access. Other places were impossible. Fallen trees lay across the creek, their tangled branches reaching down into the water. You couldn't see well enough to make out what was hidden within their grasp, or get close enough to them to feel around. If my camera was trapped beneath such a tree, it would be there forever.

I decided it was a good time to take a break. Perched on one of the many boulders lining the creek, Spud and I waited for the boys to catch up. We rested and ate a small lunch before continuing downstream. Not far from where we rested lay a bar of small, round river rock, spanning thirty yards down the center of the creek. Like most of the area we explored, the gravel bar would have been under water a good three feet or more at the time my camera was lost. My eyes scanned piles of smooth river rock. How much time and force did it take to form each rock into the smooth, round shapes beneath our feet? The ponderings of nature's many wonders were cut short as I caught sight of something out of the ordinary. It was too dark and too perfectly round to be a rock. I walked over to the object and bent down to pick it up. It was one of the lenses from my digital camera! The lens cap was still on! How bizarre. The boys raced to my side with transformed excitement. Garet reached into the water and shouted. "Look...here's the film!" He didn't realize the camera was digital and didn't take film. What he did find, however, was one of the yellow AA NiCd rechargeable batteries the camera used for power. We had found the proverbial "needle in a haystack." Finding an entire package of needles should be a walk in the park! With renewed eagerness, we searched the surrounding area until the sun began to disappear behind the mountain. Cold and wet, but with a renewed sense of hope, we crawled out of the creek and headed back to camp.

The boys were less than enthusiastic over the prospect of spending another day crawling around in the creek. Blake wanted to fish; and Garet preferred exploring the surrounding ruins. Reluctantly both boys followed me back into the creek, close to the same spot where we found the lens and battery. We quickly fell into the same order as the previous day's search: Blake fishing, Garet skipping rocks, and Spud following my every step. I crawled in and out of the water, often on hands and knees in water up to my neck.

We continued in this manner for most of the day, without a trace of the lost camera. Blake's constant complaining was getting on my nerves. He was wearing those baggy jeans boys his age seem to think are "so cool." His jeans were soaked, causing them to ride down around his ankles. He spent half of his time tripping over his pants, and the other half, pulling them up.

The pack station was only two or three hundred feet downstream. "We will get out there," I told them. Just as we headed toward the bank, I glanced over to the other side of the creek. I had to blink several times before I realized what I was seeing. Caught on a small limb sticking out of the creek's bank was my blue canvas camera bag! I could tell by the way the bag bobbed up and down that the camera was not inside. The bag collapsed in my hands as water spilled back into the creek. Every compartment of the blue canvas bag was unzipped; its contents, nowhere to be seen. Even my fishing license, in its waterproof Ziploc baggy, was gone; and with it, hope of someone finding the camera and returning it to the rightful owner…gone. We combed the immediate area, in case the camera had fallen out nearby. We came up empty-handed. As we walked to the pack station in defeat, any hopes of finding my camera totally disappeared. If we hadn't found it by now, we never would. The creek was littered with too much impenetrable debris. If the camera had made it this far, then surely someone picked it up. Maybe they found the bag, took the camera, and tossed the bag back into the creek. Maybe it had floated downstream ten more miles…twenty miles. Maybe it floated clear to the Snake River. I had had enough; we packed up our little trailer, and headed for home.

Apparently, I had issues with letting go. I felt like a pit bull that had grabbed hold of something and wouldn't let go until my jaws were pried open with a crowbar. The nagging feeling that my camera was still in that creek somewhere haunted me. I was becoming disturbingly obsessed! Like a detective at a crime scene, I went over the clues in my head at least a million times. I had a lens, a battery, and a bag, all found within one hundred yards of each other. The bag had obviously come unzipped, spilling its contents along the way before it became snagged on the limb. Questions whirled in my mind: Did the lens and battery fall out first since they were the smallest? When did the camera actually fall out? Did the camera stay in the bag, and fall out after it became snagged? Or did it fall out between the lens and the battery? We had searched the entire area with a fine-tooth comb. If the camera was between the bag and the lens, surely I would have found it. I decided the camera stayed in the bag until it was snagged, eventually working its way out. Yep, that's what happened. My camera was somewhere between the pack station and the Pacific Ocean.

PART IV
The Final Search

o o o o o o o o o o o o o o o o o o o o o o o o o o o o o o o o

Sometimes you have to take a step back in order to discover what's been right under your feet all along.

—L. A. B.

October 2, 2004: David had a week of vacation time on the books. Normally, he would have gone hunting. This time he wanted to go back to search for my camera. At first I didn't want to waste our time. God knows everyone else kept insisting I would never find the camera. I decided to humor David and go along for the ride. Ignoring the pessimistic majority, I e-mailed my counter part in Salem that I would be taking a few days off. He asked where I was going and how long I would be gone. I said, "I'm going to find my camera. I won't be back until I do." I thought I was being facetious.

David, Blake, Spud, and I drove to the pack station for the last time. Whether we found the camera or not was irrelevant. This was the last time we would be able to drive into the trailhead. Once the snow hit, the entire mountain would be impassable until spring. I decided that, in order to deal with my "letting go" issues, I should formulate a plan. We would start at the spot where I was standing three months ago when my camera hit the water. We would walk down the creek to the bridge at Cornucopia, and that would be the end of it. I would convince myself I had done everything humanly possible to find my camera. Whatever the outcome, I would accept it, get over it, and get on with life.

We stood where the trail meets the water's edge, shaking our heads at the sight; the creek was a mere trickle of its former self. The water was as low as it would get before winter set in. No one would have imagined just three short months ago, the creek had been so high, and moving so fast, that crossing was nearly impossible. But we knew; oh, how we knew! We now stepped into water that barely trickled over the tops of our shoes. David walked down the right side, and I took the left. Blake, who apparently learned a lesson from his last encounter with the creek, walked down the middle in his shorts.

I now know the bends of this creek better than the back of my own hand. I know every hole, every rock, and every dead tree that lay across it. I brought a flashlight, hoping I might be able to see farther back into the eroded cutouts of the bank. Some of the cutouts were as deep as caves. It was discouraging to shine the flashlight into their dark recesses. Had the camera washed into any one of them, seeing or reaching it would be impossible. Still, we continued down the creek with ease. Blake soon became bored and began to complain. In an attempt to keep him motivated, I told him I would pay a reward of $500 to whoever spotted the camera first. I told him if I spotted the camera first, I would buy us a four-wheeler, or take us all to Hawaii. Heck, maybe I would buy a four-wheeler *and* go to Hawaii. I could have promised the moon and felt confident I never would have to pay up.

Around bend after bend, we continued our search. An hour or two later, we reached the spot where the lens was found. We stopped to rest and eat a bite of lunch. Bellies full, we resumed the search downstream. Just past the bar of river rock was a tangled mass of dead tree limbs, half covering a huge, cave-like hole, the water had eroded from the bank. I thought to myself, "If I were a camera floating precariously down the river…that is where I would be." I took my flashlight and explored the tangled mass. It was sort of creepy under there. I imagined a miniature Pine Creek version of the Loch Ness monster lurking in the depths. I reached as far back into the hole as I could without getting my head wet. Water rose past my shoulder and filled my ear. I felt around in the dark, murky water. Something cold and slimy brushed the top of my hand. I jerked back, nearly toppling over backward into the creek. Was it a snake? Did it bite me? If my camera was in that murky, monster-infested lair, it could damn well stay there.

Approximately halfway between the gravel bar where I found the lens and the spot where the bag had hung up on the limb, I turned to look back. I do not know what made me turn…maybe just to make sure whatever was in the cave wasn't coming after me. Whatever the reason, I turned around and happened to look down. I am not sure how long I stood looking down before I was able to form the words, swirling surrealistically, in my head. Ever so softly, the words spilled from my lips: "There is my camera." Face down in less than an inch of water, and half-buried in sand, was my $900 Olympus DC 5050 digital camera. I couldn't move. I couldn't do anything other than stand there like a complete idiot, pointing at my feet. I was afraid to touch it, as if doing so would make it disappear. As soon as David and Blake realized what was going on, they immediately rushed over. Still pointing at my feet and barely able to believe what I was seeing, I mumbled, "There it is…right there…I almost stepped on it." I slowly reached for the camera, and lifted it from the water. I clutched the battered piece of metal and plastic in my arms like a precious newborn, afraid to take my eyes off the thing I had searched so long to find. All at once and without warning, it hit me. With pure, uninhibited elation, I threw back my head, opened my mouth, and screamed, "*Yes! I found my camera!*" I'm normally not the type to succumb to "girlie" screaming, but scream I did. With complete, unadulterated delight, I screamed at the top of my lungs. I can honestly say it was the happiest moment in my entire life.

I turned the camera over and over in my hands. Water and sand filled every crevice. In various spots the paint was chipped, exposing the bare metal. The function dial was missing and the LCD screen was cracked. Other than those minor imperfections, the camera was surprisingly intact. I couldn't help but chuckle at the sight of the lens cap, still faithfully covering the lens. I held my breath and opened the cover that housed the memory card. The 128 megabyte xD-Picture Card was still inside. Even the release worked properly as it engaged, and the card ejected. I had no way of knowing if the card was damaged or not. Other than a small spot of corrosion forming on the contacts, the card looked like the day I bought it. I wrapped the card in an old bandana, stuffed it in my pocket…and prayed. It was one thing to find the camera after three months; but to hope the pictures were recoverable would surely be too much.

As soon as we arrived home, I cleaned what corrosion I could from the contacts and wrapped the xD Picture Card in a paper towel. I hoped doing so would draw out any moisture inside. Once again I searched the Internet for any information on water-damaged xD Picture Cards. My search revealed only a few accounts of cards immediately retrieved from water. I was afraid to try the card in a reader too soon. I wanted to give it every chance to dry before putting power to it.

Three days after finding the camera, I sat in front of my computer. David was back at work, and the boys were in school. I was alone. Lying on the desk beside my keyboard was the paper towel containing the xD-Picture Card. I took the card out and twirled it between my fingers. Aside from a tiny, pinprick-sized spot of corrosion, the card looked in perfect condition. All I had to do was insert the card into the card reader, and my questions would be answered. Could a card withstand three months underwater and still be salvageable? If so, would the pictures be as good as I had hoped? There was no time like the present to find out. It was time. I inserted the card into a USB card reader and held my breath. The little green LED light flashed twice before it stabilized to a continuous glow. A few seconds later, the "Removable Disk (F:)" drive opened to display the root folder "DCIM." The card was still readable. My heart was pounding. All I had to do was to double click on the "DCIM" folder, and the fate of my obsession would be revealed. Here was the moment of truth.

What if the pictures were not as good as I had imagined? Would I be disappointed in the shots I had taken? Was this even the actual card that contained our entire trip? What if I filled the card just before reaching the creek and had put in another? What if the card containing the pictures was still in the creek? What if Bigfoot found the camera, took pictures over top of all of mine, and only fuzzy images of a hairy, manlike beast, unfit even for the *National Inquirer*, were left? Stop it! This is ridiculous! It is now, or never. I doubled clicked the DCIM folder and stared at the screen in anticipation. Testimony of our spring adventure began to spread across my computer screen in stunning resolution. One by one, each picture drew painstakingly slow across my monitor. There was Spud, rolling around in the first patch of snow. There was the little frog pond. A picture of Dillon and David warming themselves around a small fire caused me to relive the night we endured the storm at "Satan's Camp from Hell." There was the picture of Dillon standing precariously atop the cornice overhang. There were pictures of the lake itself, blue water and crisp, white snow, framed by mountains splattered with pine trees and granite. Tears came to my eyes as the last picture appeared…there, overlooking the lake, was my ever-faithful companion, Spud. It was perfect. They were all there; and they were as awesome as I had imagined.

Epilogue

✦

A true Cornucopia

I burned several copies of the pictures to CD-ROM as backup. I was taking no chances. David, in the meantime, replaced my Olympus DC5050 with the newer model Olympus C-5060.

I keep the Olympus DC-5050 as a battered reminder of our journey. It stands to remind me not only of our adventure that spring, but as a reminder of lessons learned. I have learned it does not matter how insignificant an event may seem to others. If it is big enough to change your perspective of life, then that is what really matters. I have learned a person can go a long way on determination, a lot of hope, and a little luck. Most importantly, I have learned no matter how tall the mountain, severe the storm, or swift the current…never, ever give up.

Each of us seeks riches in our own way. Some have mined gold from the streams and mountains. Others find wealth in building communities with homes, churches, and schools for their children. I have found my true bounty within the journey itself…a journey that may have seemed no more dramatic than a bowl of green Jell-O to some, but, nonetheless, life altering for three people and a big white dog.

978-0-595-38480-8
0-595-38480-3